I'll never forget the day a RYA Instructor came to my sailing club in Scotland to run a weekend course.

It was the first time I had gone sailing without my father and the feeling of freedom and accomplishment on completing the course was amazing. I was even awarded a RYA certificate, which I passed with distinction.

Rightly or wrongly, I took this as a sign that I might have some talent. I was enthralled and took up sailing with gusto. Like all children, I loved collecting the certificates!

The RYA National Sailing Scheme and Youth Sailing Scheme ensure that you learn safely and at your own pace. They have evolved over the years from a vast wealth of experience. They demystify our sport and allow you to reach achievable goals and have fun while you are learning.

I love dinghy sailing even after all this time, and each day I sail I am still learning something new.

I hope you enjoy your RYA course and wish you all good sailing.

Have fun.

Shirley Robertson MBE
Olympic Gold Medallist 2000 & 2004

The RYA is committed to encouraging both women and men to participate in sailing.
For clarity only, this book is written using the masculine gender e.g. man overboard.

1 | How to Start Sailing

Where can you sail?

Britain is rich in places to sail. You will find sailing clubs and boating facilities on many lakes, gravel pits, reservoirs and rivers, as well as in superb coastal sailing areas. You can also take a course during a holiday at a RYA Recognised Centre overseas.

Singlehanded dinghies, like these Picos, are fun to sail and offer a quick way to learn the basics.

Learning in a dinghy is a great way to start sailing. Dinghies have simple equipment, are easy to prepare for sailing, and are light to handle.

They respond quickly to your movements so it's easy to see the effect of your actions and to feel the reaction from the boat. Dinghies used for teaching are usually fairly stable and simple, but they are still rewarding and challenging to sail.

Starting in a singlehanded dinghy can be the quickest way to learn, but on the other hand, you may enjoy learning with others in a boat designed to be sailed by two or more people; the choice is yours.

The Laser Stratos is typically sailed by two, but has room for more.

Keelboats

A **keelboat** has a weighted keel under the hull which prevents it capsizing.

Keelboats are larger than dinghies and are usually sailed by a number of people. They are stable and dry and often more comfortable to sail.

Because of their greater size and weight they do not offer the fast response and instant feedback of dinghies and the equipment tends to be heavier.

The International Sonar is typical of a day sailing and racing keelboat and is sailed by four people.

Multihulls

Most multihulls are **catamarans** (two hulls). Although catamarans and **trimarans** (three hulls) are very stable compared with dinghies, they can still capsize if allowed to **heel** (lean over) too far.

The combination of stability and light weight means that multihulls are very fast and offer exhilarating sailing.

Most catamarans are designed to be sailed by two people but there are several types that are sailed singlehanded.

Multihulls require slightly different techniques to boats with a single hull.

The Dart 16 is a very popular catamaran that can be sailed by one or two people.

1 | Clothing & Personal Equipment

Staying comfortable

There is no need to be cold and wet when you are sailing. Modern sailing clothing is warm and comfortable, providing good freedom of movement. Use thermal or fleece clothing for inner layers. Avoid cotton which is cold to wear when damp. Pick your clothing to suit when and where you sail. Even in summer it is nearly always colder on the water than ashore, and the temperature is likely to fluctuate more. Plan to wear sufficient clothing to ensure you do not get chilled. Once you are cold it can be hard to warm up again and heat loss is accelerated if your skin is wet and exposed to evaporation so wear a set of waterproofs if necessary. Staying warm is usually associated with staying dry, and most types of outer layer sailing clothing aim to keep water away from the inner layers and your skin. Alternatively, accept that you will get wet and use a wetsuit to insulate your body. This can be complimented by a waterproof top.

Wetsuits are a sensible choice when you are likely to get wet.

Waterproof jacket and trousers are ideal on a keelboat or stable dinghy.

Drysuits are often worn by sailors in high performance dinghies.

Picking the right clothing

When you start learning, a simple waterproof jacket and trousers will usually suffice and will often be provided by your sailing school. Alternatively, you may be provided with a wetsuit.

When buying your own gear, take into consideration when and where you sail. Good waterproofs plus thermal inner layers are suitable for stable dinghies or keelboats but think about using a wetsuit for faster dinghies or catamarans, especially in the winter.

If you sail fast boats, a drysuit which uses neck, ankle and wrist seals keeps all water out. However, overheating can be a problem so, if possible, pick a breathable type.

Personal safety gear

Personal safety gear is essential.

A buoyancy aid is designed to help a conscious person stay afloat if they fall overboard or the boat capsizes. A buoyancy aid is usually the most appropriate choice for dinghy or catamaran sailing as long as the sailor can swim.

An inflatable lifejacket is an alternative for keelboat sailors and is often fitted with a safety harness to prevent the person falling overboard. In the water, an inflated lifejacket will support an unconscious person and should turn them on to their back with their face clear of the water.

Always wear a buoyancy aid or a lifejacket when you go afloat.

A safety harness, often combined with a lifejacket, is used aboard keelboats.

Remember the extremities - boots, gloves and hat are all important.

TOP TIP
Most heat loss occurs through the top of the head so wear a warm hat when sailing in cold weather.

1 | Parts of the Boat

Understanding the language
You only need to know a few basic terms when you start to learn and it is sufficient to know the names for the parts of the boat shown here.

Two important words are **port** and **starboard**. The port side is the left side looking forward and always remains so even if you turn round to face astern.

The term **windward** means the upwind side of the boat. **Leeward** is the downwind side of the boat.

Bow and **stern** refer to the front and back of the boat.

Sails and their parts
The simplest boats use a single sail behind the mast. This is called the **mainsail**.

Most boats have a mainsail plus another sail, the **jib**, in front of the mast. Both sails are controlled by ropes called **sheets**.

The mainsail has a **mainsheet** attached to the boom. The jib has two **jib sheets** - one for each side of the boat.

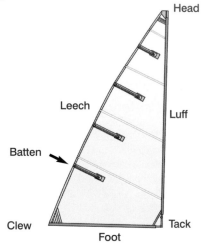

Sailing with a mainsail and jib.

Standard sails are triangular and each part has a name.

Variations on a theme
You may encounter a different mainsheet layout. Techniques will vary according to whether you sail a boat with a centre or aft mainsheet.

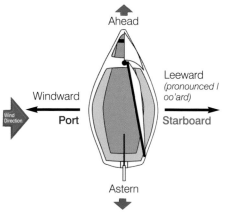

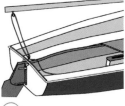

Here the mainsheet is attached at the stern - this is called an aft mainsheet.

Some directions are described relative to the boat or the wind.

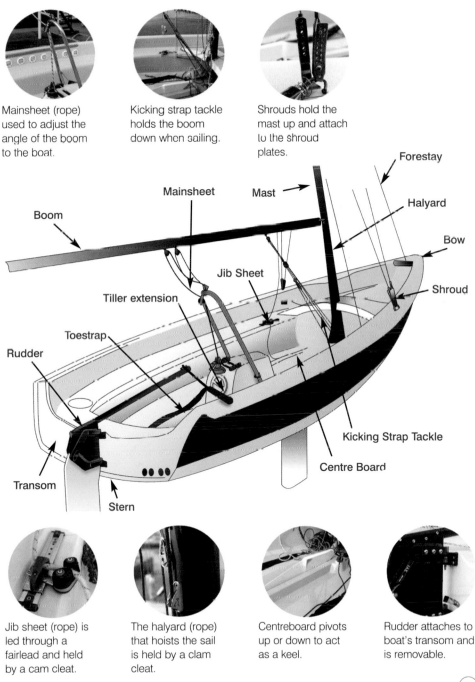

Mainsheet (rope) used to adjust the angle of the boom to the boat.

Kicking strap tackle holds the boom down when sailing.

Shrouds hold the mast up and attach to the shroud plates.

Forestay

Mainsheet   Mast

Boom

Halyard

Bow

Jib Sheet

Shroud

Tiller extension

Toestrap

Rudder

Kicking Strap Tackle

Centre Board

Transom

Stern

Jib sheet (rope) is led through a fairlead and held by a cam cleat.

The halyard (rope) that hoists the sail is held by a clam cleat.

Centreboard pivots up or down to act as a keel.

Rudder attaches to boat's transom and is removable.

1 | A Variety of Types

A singlehanded dinghy

Singlehanded dinghies are very popular because they are relatively low in cost and light in weight. As they are easy to transport, rig and launch you can arrive at a venue and go sailing within minutes.

Most singlehanded dinghies have a single sail (the **mainsail**) set on a simple mast that does not need shrouds to hold it upright.

The sail usually has a simple sleeve at the luff. The mast is slid into the sleeve. The mast is then fitted into a socket in the deck.

The controls are equally simple; the **mainsheet** controls the position of the sail, while the kicking strap holds the boom down. There are **toestraps** to tuck your feet under when sitting out, and a **tiller extension** for steering.

Most singlehanded dinghies have a **daggerboard** which slides vertically through the bottom of the boat and prevents the boat from sliding sideways. Other types of dinghy may use a pivoting centreboard which does the same job.

> **TOP TIP**
> Try out a range of boats when you start sailing to find out which type you enjoy most. Many clubs have boats available for hire.

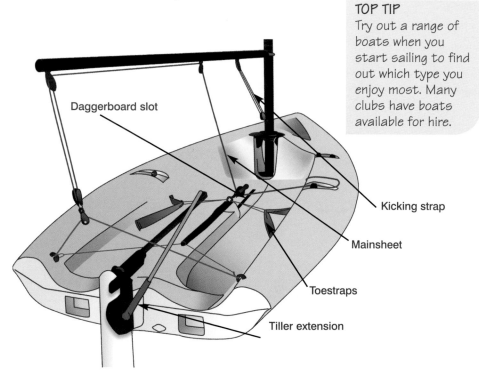

Daggerboard slot

Kicking strap

Mainsheet

Toestraps

Tiller extension

The Pico is a popular singlehander that makes a good first boat when you are learning to sail. It is easy to sail alone but can also accommodate another person if you want some company.

A small keelboat

Small keelboats are not as common as dinghies but there is still a fair selection to choose from.

All the normal equipment you would find in a dinghy will be present, except for a centreboard or daggerboard. Instead, a weighted keel gives the boat its stability. In some keelboats, the keel can be raised to make it easier to store or transport the boat ashore.

As well as the normal controls there may also be some other gear, such as winches, that make it easier to handle the larger boat.

The Sonar has a fixed keel that requires a special cradle or trailer for storage ashore, but it has a simple, dinghy-like layout.

A catamaran

Catamarans have two hulls, which are connected by crossbeams. A fabric trampoline is laced to the two crossbeams and hulls, providing a large area for the crew. Many catamarans use a loose-footed mainsail without a boom. The mainsheet is attached directly to the clew of the sail. The mast partially rotates which makes the mainsail more efficient.

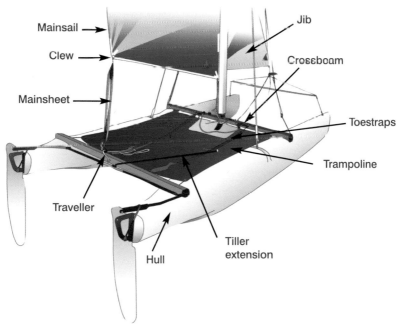

Mainsail
Clew
Mainsheet
Traveller
Hull
Jib
Crossbeam
Toestraps
Trampoline
Tiller extension

The Dart 16 is typical of many small catamarans.
It has exciting performance and is suitable for both learning and racing.

1 | Rigging your Boat

Preparing the boat for sailing

The process of attaching and hoisting sails is known as **rigging** the boat. For your first sail, an instructor or experienced sailor will show you how to attach the sails in readiness for **hoisting** them before you go afloat. The different types of dinghies, keelboats and catamarans all have their own ways of attaching and hoisting sails but the principles remain the same.

Step 1 Attach the jib tack to the bow.

Step 2 Lead the jib sheets through their fairleads (guides for ropes).

Step 3 Attach the jib halyard.

Step 4 Fasten the mainsail tack to the boom.

Step 5 Fasten the outhaul to the mainsail. Step 6 (No picture) attach the mainsail halyard.

Using a launching trolley

Most dinghies and catamarans have launching trolleys built to suit their shape. Always tie the bow of the boat to the trolley handle to prevent it sliding off, and make sure the boat is sitting correctly on the supports before moving it.

Take care when moving a boat on a trolley. Always look up to make sure the mast does not hit overhead obstructions, such as power cables. Be careful not to lose control when going down a slipway. If the mainsail is hoisted, leave the kicking strap slack to de-power the sail.

Use a trolley that gives good support to the boat and tie the dinghy to the handle to prevent it sliding off until you are ready to launch.

Hoisting sails

It is generally easier to hoist sails ashore but this will depend on the wind direction and strength.

The key points to remember are:

- Hoist the jib first. Provided the sheets are loose, it will flap freely. The jib can usually be hoisted before launching.

- The mainsheet and the kicking strap must be completely slack before hoisting the mainsail.

- Point the boat exactly into the wind before hoisting the mainsail so that it can flap freely.

Step 1 Feed the luff into the mast groove and pull on the halyard.

- To make launching easier you may choose to hoist the mainsail once the boat is afloat.

Step 2 If the mainsail jams, stop pulling and make sure the luff is able to slide smoothly into the luff groove.

Step 3 On dinghies with a removable boom, attach the boom to the mast after hoisting the mainsail.

Partially roll the mainsail around the mast to reef a singlehanded dinghy.

Reducing sail area

In order to maintain control in strong winds it may be necessary to reduce the amount of sail you use. This is called **reefing**.

Most singlehanded dinghies can be reefed by rolling the sail around the mast. Two-person dinghies with aft mainsheet systems can usually be reefed by rolling the mainsail around the boom.

Whatever method your boat uses, it is easier to reef ashore than afloat. If in doubt, put in a reef before you launch. You can take the reef out afloat, if you find you do not need it.

TOP TIP Before hoisting the mainsail turn the boat directly into the wind, and release the kicking strap and mainsheet.

2 | Your First Time Afloat

Launching the boat

Wheel the boat on its trolley to the launching point.

- Check that you have all the equipment you need.
- Check that there is a paddle in the boat.
- Ensure that all the bungs are in place, sealing the buoyancy compartments.
- Attach the rudder and tiller.
- If your boat uses a daggerboard, make sure that it is in the boat.
- Check that your buoyancy aid is secure.

Now you are ready to go:

- Wheel the boat stern first into the water until it floats off its trolley.
- Undo the rope securing the boat to the trolley handle.
- Hold the boat by its bow and allow it to swing round to point into the wind.
- Pull the trolley clear of the water and park it out of the way of other slipway users.

Getting away from the shore

On your first sail you will use a safe open area where you can learn your basic skills. Check the wind direction before you sail away, the jib is a useful indicator. Once sailing it is all too easy to focus inside the boat, so remember to keep a good lookout at all times.

Hold the trolley by the handle and wheel the boat stern first into the water.

Push the boat into deeper water until it floats off its trolley.

Catamarans use an axle with two wheels and hull supports - hold the bows to push the boat.

With the boat head to wind, one person holds the bow and the other hoists the mainsail.

Paddling and rowing

Sometimes it is easier to paddle or row away from the shore than to sail; the launching area may be constricted or the wind could be blowing directly onto the shore, making it difficult to sail off.

Few modern dinghies are equipped for rowing but it is worth carrying at least one paddle in case the wind drops.

One person paddles while the other steers.

If you are paddling, sit forwards by the shrouds. In a singlehanded dinghy you can sit on the tiller extension to steer while you paddle, or use a one-handed paddle.

If your boat is equipped for rowing then practice the skill in a clear stretch of water away from obstructions.

Rowing is a satisfying skill to learn.

Steering a sailing boat

Once your boat is away from the shore in clear water you will be able to start steering under sail. The person who steers is called the **helmsman** - this is not gender-specific, it's simply a traditional name - while the others on board are called the **crew**.

The helmsman sits on the windward side of the boat forward of the the tiller and holds the tiller extension in his rear hand. In a two-person boat the crew sits just forward of the helmsman.

On your first sail you will learn how to steer the boat using the tiller extension.
Push or pull on the tiller extension and the rudder will turn to change the boat's course.

In a boat with a centre mainsheet, hold the tiller extension in a dagger grip with the end across your body.

With an aft mainsheet use a pan handle grip and hold the extension beside your body.

In a catamaran use a dagger grip with the extension over your aft shoulder.

TOP TIP You can only steer a car when it is moving - a boat is the same and if it slows down too much it will not respond to the tiller.

2 | Understanding how a Boat Works

How sails work

To understand how a sail works, try a simple experiment with a spoon under a running tap. Hold the spoon lightly by the handle and move the back of the spoon slowly towards the stream of water. You would expect it to be pushed away by the water but actually the spoon is sucked into the flow.

The same thing happens when air flows around a sail. The air travelling around the outside (leeward side) of the sail moves faster round the sail than the air on the windward side. This causes a difference in pressure on the two sides of the sail which pulls the sail to leeward. The force created by the sail acts roughly at right angles to the boom but only part of it drives the boat forward - the rest tries to push it sideways.

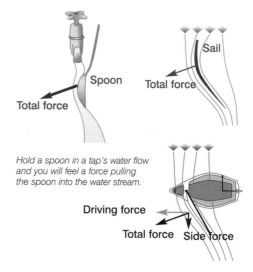

Hold a spoon in a tap's water flow and you will feel a force pulling the spoon into the water stream.

Trimming sails

A sail works best when its leading edge (**the luff**) is held at a small angle to the wind. The angle is quite critical but there is a simple way to find it. Watch the luff of the sail as you pull in the sheet. Stop pulling when the luff stops shaking. To check that the sail is properly trimmed, slowly let out the sheet until the luff starts to shake, then pull it in again until the shaking stops. Most jibs and some mainsails have **telltales**. These are fitted near the luff, on each side of the sail and help to trim the sail accurately.

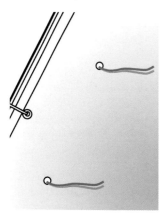

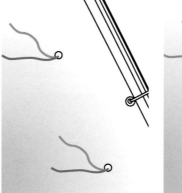

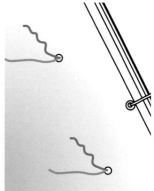

When both telltales stream back together the sail is set perfectly.

If the leeward telltale (here the red one) flutters let the sail out a little.

If the windward telltale (here the green one) flutters pull in the sail until it stops.

How keels work

A boat's keel, centreboard, or daggerboard is designed to resist the sideways force created by the sails (the rudder also plays a part).

When the boat starts to move, water flows across the keel in much the same way as air flows across the sail. It creates a sideways force to windward that resists the opposite force on the sail. The two sideways forces cancel each other out leaving a forward force which drives the boat.

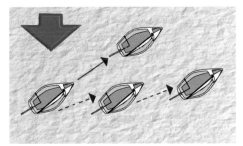

If the centreboard is not lowered sufficiently the boat will slip sideways on upwind courses.

The force on the sails acts roughly at right angles to the boom. With sails in tight (when sailing close to the wind) the force acts mainly in a sideways direction. More sideways resistance is therefore required from the keel. This is why most dinghies and some catamarans have a lifting centreboard or daggerboard, so that the area under the boat can be adjusted to suit the **point of sailing**.

The dinghy's crew sit out to balance the heeling force and keep the boat upright.

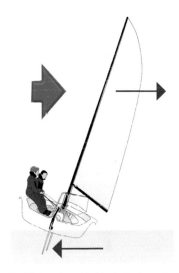

The sail's side force is resisted by the keel, causing the boat to heel. This has to be balanced by the crew's weight.

Staying upright

The force created by the sail acts above the boat. Similarly, the force created by the keel acts under the boat. These two opposing forces, acting a long way apart, create a heeling force that will cause the boat to capsize if it is not resisted.

Keelboats use the weight of a fixed keel to keep them upright, while dinghies and catamarans rely on the weight and position of the crew.

TOP TIP All sails work best when they are pulled in only just enough to stop the flapping at the luff - any more will slow the boat down.

2 | The Points of Sailing

Sailing across the wind

One of the delights of sailing is that the boat is completely reliant on the wind. This means that you must be aware of the wind direction and also its strength.

- On your first sail you will start by steering on a **beam reach** with the wind coming over the side of the boat. This is the easiest point of sailing on which to practice steering the boat.

- You can sail in two directions on a beam reach - on **port tack** when the wind comes over the port side, and on **starboard tack** when the wind comes across the starboard side.

- On a beam reach the sails are set about halfway out. Lower the centreboard about halfway down to resist the sideforce from the sails, which is moderate on this point of sailing.

Sailing upwind

- Turn towards the wind (**luff**) onto a **close reach**. Pull the sails in until they stop flapping. Put the centreboard three-quarters down to resist the increased side force.

- Turn further towards the wind and pull the sails in tight to sail **closehauled**. Put the centreboard fully down. This is the closest angle a sailing boat can sail to the wind. If you sail any closer the sails will start flapping and the boat will slow down. The heeling force is also greatest so sit out on the windward side to keep the boat upright.

- To sail directly upwind it is necessary to follow a zigzag course turning (**tacking**) through 90 degrees each time.

Sailing downwind

From a beam reach, turn away from the wind (**bearing away**) onto a **broad reach**.

- As you turn **downwind** let the sails out to keep them set at the correct angle to the wind. As this reduces the side force, the centreboard can be raised three quarters. Move the crew inboard.

- Bear away more, letting out the sails as you go, until the jib falls slack in the wind shadow of the mainsail. The boat is now on a **run** with the mainsail right out. Pull the centreboard almost all the way up.

- Sailing on a run can be quite confusing when you start, so luff up until the jib fills again and sail on a **training run**. This is a more stable route downwind. Sit one on either side to balance the boat.

Sailing to windward

To go upwind, sail as close to the wind as you can. Sailing closehauled efficiently means sailing on the edge of the no-go zone without turning into it.

- The crew pulls the jib in tight and can cleat the sheet.

- The helmsman steers by watching the jib telltales.

- Luff gently until the windward telltales lift then, if the boat starts to slow down, bear away until both telltales stream together. If sailing a singlehander, use the telltales on the mainsail.

Use the jib telltales to luff and bear away gently along the edge of the no-go zone.

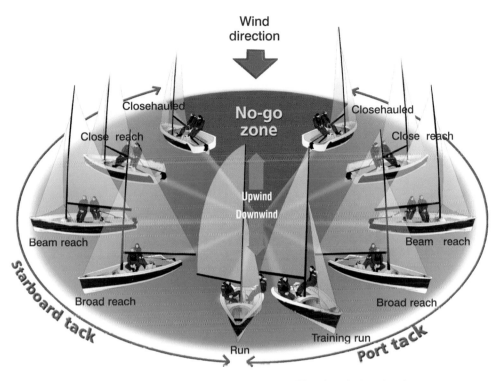

The points of sailing describe a boat's course in terms of the angle of the boat to the wind.

Tacking and gybing

When sailing upwind, to change course from port to starboard tack (or vice versa), turn the bow through the wind. This is known as tacking. When sailing downwind turn the stern through the wind. This is known as **gybing**.

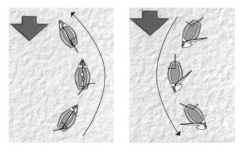

Change from one tack to the other by tacking (left) or gybing (right).

2 | First Skills

Stopping and starting

Sailing boats do not have brakes so to stop you have to make use of the wind. To do this, turn the boat onto a close reach and let out the sails until they flap. The boat will stop in the lying-to position with the sails out of your way on the leeward side.

It is also possible to stop by turning head to wind but the boat will not stay in this position for long. Use the **lying-to** position whenever you need to stop the boat temporarily. To start sailing again, pull in the sails and as the boat moves forwards, steer on to the new course.

Make sure that you are on a close reach then let the sails right out.

This keelboat is lying-to while the crew tidy up the gear before a race.

Turning the boat

Although the rudder steers the boat, this is not the only control and it is important to adjust the sails, crew position and the centreboard as you turn.

Practise turning the boat and making adjustments to the controls as you turn towards and away from the wind.

To turn away from the wind (bear away)
steer onto the new course and:

- let out the sails
- raise the centreboard
- move your weight to balance the boat

To turn towards the wind (luff) steer onto the new course and:

- pull in the sails
- lower the centreboard
- move your weight to balance the boat

The five essentials

There are five essential factors to sailing a boat efficiently. Whenever one factor changes, check the other four to make sure they are still correct.

- **Sail trim** - Constantly check that the sails are set properly by using the telltales or by slowly letting out the sails until they start to shake along the luff, then pulling them in again until the shaking just stops. This becomes second nature after a while.

- **Centreboard position** - The daggerboard or centreboard position needs to be adjusted according to the side force. The amount of side force, and hence the centreboard area, varies from maximum when closehauled to virtually zero when on a run. On a keelboat you cannot adjust the area.

- **Boat balance** - Most boats sail fastest when upright. This is achieved by the crew moving their weight to balance the boat. When sailing closehauled, the heeling force is large so the

helmsman and crew sit out to keep the boat upright. On a run, the heeling force is small so the crew moves to the opposite side of the boat to balance the helmsman's weight.

- **Boat trim** - Generally, the boat should be level fore-and-aft. Depending on the conditions, the helmsman and crew sit close together and avoid depressing the bow or stern excessively.

- **Course** - Keep checking your course and the best route to your destination. If your target is to windward anywhere in the no-go zone, you will have to zig-zag upwind to get there.

> **TOP TIP** The sails have a big turning effect so when you want to bear away let out the mainsail first. To luff up pull the mainsail in as you turn.

2 | Learning to Tack

Basic Principles

Tacking involves turning the boat so that the bow passes through the wind while the sails and the crew change sides. It requires good co-ordination between helmsman and crew: turning the boat, moving your weight to the new side, and trimming the sails. The basic principles apply to all boats but different equipment may require different techniques.

The easiest way to learn is to tack from one beam reach to the other. To tack successfully, get the boat sailing fast before the tack and hold the tiller over until the turn is complete.

Step 1

Tacking with a centre mainsheet

Step 1 Look over your shoulder and check that the area is clear of other boats.

Call **"Ready about"** to warn the crew. The crew also checks that the area is clear, uncleats the jib sheet and replies,**"Ready"**. Call **"Lee-oh"** to tell the crew that the turn is starting.

Step 2

Step 2 Ease the tiller away from you, the boom will start to move into the boat. As the sail crosses the boat, hold the end of the tiller extension ahead of you and move across the boat, facing forward. Ease the sheet a little. Keep looking forward and hold the tiller over until the sail starts to fill on the other side.

Step 3

Step 3 Turn to sit down on the new side, holding the extension behind your back.

Step 4 Once the boat is on course, straighten the tiller, bring the hand holding the mainsheet to the tiller hand and swap hands on the sheet and extension. Trim the sails as necessary. Tidy up the sheet falls.

Tacking with an aft mainsheet

Tacking a boat with an aft mainsheet is slightly different: change hands on the mainsheet and tiller extension before the tack, and cross the boat facing the stern. To do this:

Step 1 Look over your shoulder and check that the area is clear of other boats. Call "Ready about" then change hands on the tiller extension and the mainsheet. Hold the extension in the new hand and ease the tiller away, calling "Lee-oh".

Step 2 Put your front foot across the boat and pivot to move into the middle of the boat facing aft.

Step 3 As the boom passes over your head turn to sit down on the new side and straighten the tiller as the sail fills. Trim the sails. Tidy up the sheet falls.

The crew's role

The crew's job during the tack is to check for obstructions and to move across the boat while setting the jib on the new side.

Step 1 When the helmsman calls "Ready about", check that the area is clear, uncleat the jib sheet and reply "Ready".

Step 2 Aim to be in the middle of the boat at the same time as the boom. As the boat turns and the jib starts to flap let go of the old jib sheet and pick up the new one.

Step 3 When the jib has blown across to the new side, pull in the sheet to trim the jib for the new course and balance the boat.

> **TOP TIP** When tacking or gybing a centre mainsheet boat face forward and change hands after the tack. In an aft mainsheet boat change hands first and face aft.

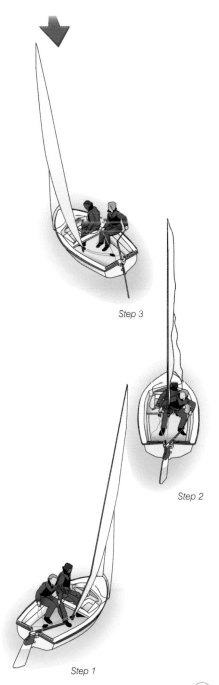

Step 3

Step 2

Step 1

2 | Learning to Tack

Tacking a catamaran

Tacking a catamaran requires a slightly different technique. A catamaran's light weight and wide beam causes the boat to stop quickly when it comes head to wind in the middle of the tack. To prevent this, make sure the boat is sailing fast on a closehauled course before the tack.

The helmsman's role

The preparatory checks and commands to the crew are the same as in a single-hull dinghy:

Step 1 To start the tack, push the tiller extension to turn the rudders to an angle of about 45°. At the same time, sheet in the mainsail tightly to help the boat turn into the wind.

Step 2 Move into the middle and kneel on the trampoline, facing aft. As the mainsheet traveller moves into the centre, rotate the tiller extension aft behind the mainsheet. Pass it to the other side and change hands on the mainsheet and extension.

Step 3 As soon as the boat passes head to wind, ease the mainsheet a little. Bear away slightly and sheet in until the boat picks up speed, then luff back to closehauled.

The crew's role

When the boat turns head to wind, allow the jib to back a little (**backing the jib**). This will help the boat turn through the wind without stopping. As the mainsail fills, release the windward sheet and pull in the sail on the leeward side. Move across the boat to the new windward side.

Step 1

Step 2

Step 3

> **TOP TIP** In a boat with a jib, the crew can help recover from in-irons by pulling the jib sheet on the side opposite the boom - called backing the jib.

Tacking a singlehanded dinghy

Good timing and smooth movements are the key to tacking a singlehanded dinghy. Most have a centre mainsheet arrangement, so you tack facing forwards. Being small and light singlehanded dinghies turn quickly.

At first, aim to tack fairly slowly until you get used to the routine.

Step 1

Step 2

Step 1 Check the area is clear, push the tiller gently away, ease the mainsheet as the boat turns head to wind to give yourself a little time. Don't move across the boat until the boom approaches the centreline, with the boat heeled slightly towards you.

Step 2 The boom is often low so duck to get under it as you cross the boat. Move across quickly and get your weight onto the new windward side, centralise the tiller as the boat completes the tack.

Step 3 Sit out to balance the boat, and pull the mainsheet back in as the boat comes upright. Change hands on mainsheet and tiller extension after the tack then sheet in the mainsheet and resume a closehauled course. Keep the sheet falls tidy.

Step 3

In-irons

When a boat stops head to wind, usually during a failed tack, it is **in-irons**. The rudder has no effect because the boat is not moving through the water. To recover from this situation push the tiller away from you and push the boom away to back the mainsail. The boat will move backwards and turn away from the wind. Now pull on the tiller and pull on the mainsheet to get the boat sailing again.

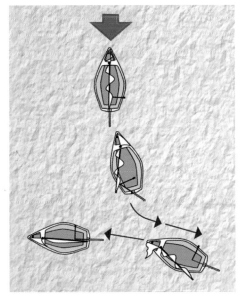

If you get stuck in-irons remember the solution: PUSH PUSH then PULL PULL.

2 | Learning to Gybe

Basic principles

Gybing takes the boat from one tack to the other when sailing downwind by turning the stern through the wind. During a gybe, the sails stay full throughout. Gybing happens more quickly than tacking, and the boom swings across the boat more forcefully. Balance the boat throughout the gybe or it may capsize. Raise the centreboard or daggerboard three- quarters up to reduce the heeling effect.

Step 1

Step 2

Step 3

Step 4

Centre mainsheet gybing

Always face forward when gybing a centre mainsheet boat.

Step 1 Bear away until the jib hangs limply behind the   mainsail, then luff up to a training run. This is the best starting point when you are learning to gybe. Check the area is clear and pull the boom off the leeward shroud. Check the centreboard is three- quarters up. Call **"Stand by to gybe"**. Swing the tiller extension round to the leeward side. Place your aft foot across the boat, moving to the middle.

Step 2 Call **"Gybe-oh"** to warn the crew, then push the tiller to windward. Watch the leech of the mainsail just above the boom; when it starts to curl, the boat is on the point of gybing. Be ready to duck under the boom and pull on the mainsheet falls to start the boom swinging across. As the boom crosses the centreline smoothly centralise the tiller to stop the turn.

Step 3 Move smartly across and sit down on the new side, steering with the extension held behind your back.

Step 4 Change hands on the extension and mainsheet to finish the gybe. Trim the sails as necessary. Tidy sheet falls.

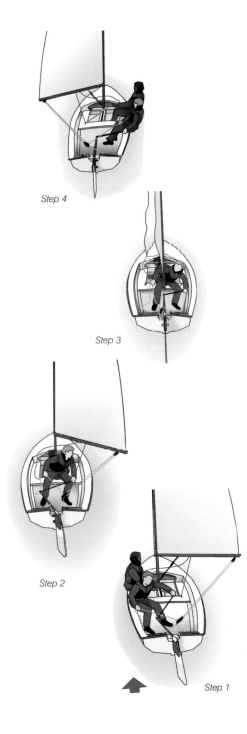

Step 4

Step 3

Step 2

Step 1

Aft mainsheet gybing

Gybing with an aft mainsheet is slightly different. As with tacking, change hands on the mainsheet and tiller extension before the gybe and cross the boat facing aft.

Step 1 Do the pre-gybe checks, including checking the area is clear and warn the crew you are about to gybe by calling "**Stand by to Gybe**". Change hands on the mainsheet and extension. Call "**Gybe-oh**" and push the tiller to windward to start the turn.

Step 2 Move to the middle of the boat, facing aft. Be ready to duck to avoid the boom. Watch the leech of the mainsail just above the boom; when it starts to curl, the boat is on the point of gybing. Give a tug on the mainsheet to start the boom moving.

Step 3 Centralise the tiller to stop the boat turning as the boom crosses the centreline.

Step 4 Sit down on the new side and trim the sails. Tidy sheet falls.

The crew's role

The crew's main job during a gybe is to balance the boat while sheeting the jib to the new side. Before the gybe, check for obstructions and check the centreboard position. When the jib blows to the new side, release the old sheet and pull in the new leeward one. As in tacking, the crew should be in the middle of the boat as the boom swings across and be ready to balance the boat after the turn.

TOP TIP Make sure that the boat is upright before the gybe. If it heels to leeward it will be much harder to gybe as the boat will try to turn the wrong way.

2 | Learning to Gybe

Gybing a catamaran

It is usually easier to gybe a catamaran than a single-hull dinghy because its greater stability means that there is less chance of a capsize. However, its extra speed means that you need plenty of room to manoeuvre and the boat should be under full control before you start the gybe.

Step 1

Step 2

Step 3

Step 4

The helmsman's role

The checks and warnings for the crew are the same as in a single-hull dinghy. If your catamaran has centreboards or daggerboards they should be fully raised.

Step 1 Start the gybe by pulling the tiller extension to turn the rudders.

Step 2 Move to the middle of the boat as the boat turns onto a run and kneel, facing aft. Keep the rudders over to continue the turn and rotate the tiller extension aft. Swing the tiller extension behind the mainsheet to the other side and change hands on the mainsheet and extension.

Step 3 With your new mainsheet hand, grasp the mainsheet falls. As the sail swings across, briefly check the mainsheet's movement to leeward. This will cause the sail's full-length battens to 'pop' across on the new tack. Straighten the rudders.

Step 4 Sit down on the windward hull and steer onto your new course.

The crew's role

A catamaran's stability makes it easy for the crew to balance the boat. Before the gybe, check that the route is clear. If your boat has centreboards or daggerboards make sure that they are raised. Respond with "Ready", uncleat the old jib sheet and pick up the new one. When the jib crosses to the new side, release the jib sheet, pull in the other one, and move to the new windward side.

Step 1

Step 2

Step 3

Step 4

Gybing a singlehanded dinghy

In a singlehanded dinghy you have sole responsibility for balancing the boat. Plan your gybe in advance. The end of the low boom may hit the water when it swings across which could result in a capsize, so ease the kicking strap a little before the gybe, to let the boom lift and reduce the risk. Also, pull the daggerboard nearly all the way up, but not so far that the top could be snagged by the kicking strap during the gybe. (If this happens a capsize is certain).

The faster you go the easier it is to gybe, so wait until the boat is moving well. When sailing in waves, this is when the boat accelerates down a wave face.

Most singlehanded dinghies have a centre mainsheet so gybe facing forward.

Step 1 Steer onto a run and swing the end of the tiller extension round to point across the boat, then push the tiller to windward.

Step 2 Move into the middle of the boat ready to gybe.

Step 3 Watch the leech and when it curls tug on the mainsheet to help the boom across.

Step 4 Move to the new side and change hands.

Developing wind awareness

It is much easier to learn key manoeuvres if you develop a good awareness of wind direction. The wind is constantly changing so check its direction regularly. While flags ashore, or smoke from chimneys give a general idea of wind direction, most dinghies have a wind indicator at the masthead. String tied to the shrouds will give you an eye level guide. The best indicator is the feel of wind on your face and neck and the set of the sails. With a little practise, you will soon develop an automatic awareness of wind direction.

2 | Knots and Ropework

Introduction

Ropes are an essential part of a sailing boat and whilst many racing boats have quite complex control systems you only need to know a few knots to cope with most needs.

A simple passing turn (left) and a round turn (right).

Modern ropes are incredibly strong and light, and come in a wide range of sizes. Use low stretch rope for sheets, halyards and control lines. Keep the length just long enough for the job so the rope doesn't tangle.

Figure-of-eight

The figure-of-eight is used to put a stopper knot in the end of rope to stop it running out through a fairlead or turning block.

(1) Cross the end over then under the standing part and (2) pass it through the loop made by the crossing turn. Leave a long tail for security and pull to tighten.

Round turn & two half hitches

The round turn and two half hitches is a secure knot that is used to tie to a post or ring.

(1) Make a turn around the post or through the ring. (2) Pass the end around the standing part and over itself, to form a half hitch. (3) Pass the end around the standing part and over itself again to form the second half hitch. (4) Pull the end and the standing part to tighten the knot.

Bowline

The bowline is used to make a loop in a rope or to tie to a ring or post. It is a secure knot but cannot be untied when under load.

(1) Make a crossing turn and hold both parts of the rope with your fingers. (2) Roll your wrist over to form a crossing turn around your hand and the end. (3) Pass the end behind the standing part and back down through the crossing turn. (4) Pull the standing part and the doubled working end to tighten.

Clove hitch

A clove hitch can be used to tie a rope to a post or ring. It is quick to tie but a snatching load can undo it, so leave a long working end.

1 *2*

(1) Pass the end around the post and bring it over the standing part. (2) Make another turn and tuck the end under this second turn. Pull the working end and standing part to tighten.

Rolling hitch

The rolling hitch is more secure than the clove hitch and will not slide along another rope or a spar. It is useful when you need to take the load off another rope.

1 *2* *3*

(1)Make a passing turn around the spar bringing the end up over the standing part. (2) Make another identical turn, crossing over the standing part again. (3) Cross over the standing part again and make a third turn, tucking the end under the turn. (4) Pull the end and the standing part. Put strain on the standing part only in the direction of the double turns, in this case to the right.

Using a cleat

1 Take the rope to the back of the cleat and make a full turn around the cleat's base.

2 Make two or three full figure-of-eight turns around the cleat.

3 Finish by taking a full turn around the base of the cleat.

Using winches

Larger boats tend to use winches to help with the heavy loads on sheets and halyards.

(1) Wrap the rope clockwise around the winch keeping your hands well away to avoid trapping your fingers between rope and drum. (2) Put three turns on the drum then insert the handle in the winch and pull on the tail (end) while winding the handle. With two people, one person winds while the other tails.

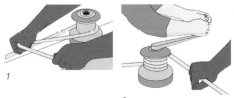

1

2

3 | Leaving and Returning to Shore

Onshore and offshore winds

Sailing to and from the shore is straightforward if you understand the importance of wind direction.The wind direction dictates the type of shore situation you will encounter. When the wind is blowing along the shore, you can easily sail away and return on a beam reach.

More often the wind blows off the shore (**windward shore**) or onto the shore (**lee shore**).

Offshore winds

It is often deceptively calm on a windward shore but there may be stronger winds offshore. Be cautious in case you start with too much sail. Launch the boat with the sails hoisted before sailing away on a broad reach or run.

To return, sail to windward to reach the shore. As the water gets shallower be ready to raise the centreboard and rudder to keep them clear of the bottom. Turn into the wind and let out the sails to stop. Step over the side when the water is waist deep or less. Hold the boat by the bow, lower the sails, and take the boat out of the water.

Offshore wind   *Onshore wind*

To leave a windward shore push the bow away and sheet in the jib as you climb aboard.

Returning to a windward shore stop the boat and step over the side into shallow water.

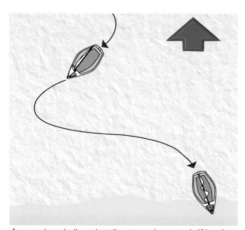

Approach a shallow shoreline on a close reach lifting the centreboard as you approach.

Onshore winds

Waves break on a lee shore in moderate or strong winds and make launching harder and recovery more difficult. If the shore line shelves steeply it may be unsafe to launch, so find a better launching site.

Before launching into deep water, turn the boat head to wind and hoist the jib. Then launch, hoisting the mainsail once afloat. In a singlehanded dinghy, rig ashore and get a friend to help you launch.

To leave a lee shore push off, climb aboard quickly and steer onto a close reach until you reach water deep enough to fully lower the centreboard and rudder. Then sail closehauled to get away from the shore.

To return to a lee shore, turn head to wind just offshore, lower the mainsail, and sail in using the jib alone. In a singlehanded dinghy, sail in and, if the bottom is gently shelving, turn head to wind near the shore and step out.

On a steeply shelving shore, sail straight in, luff sharply to de-power the sail and jump out on the windward side when the water is shallow enough. Then get the boat ashore quickly.

Under tow

To get to and from the sailing area, boats are often towed one behind the other. Lower the sails when being towed, pull the centreboard right up and remove the rudder. Sit near the stern to lift the bow. The last boat in the tow keeps its rudder fitted and steers to follow the boat directly ahead. In a singlehanded dinghy, remove the boom to allow the mainsail to flap freely or roll the sail up.

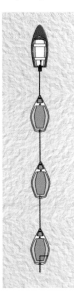

The last boat is steered to follow the boat ahead.

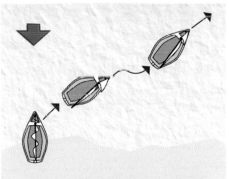

To sail off from a lee shore steer on a close reach until the water is deep enough to lower the centreboard fully.

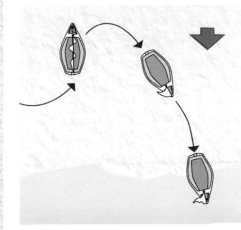

To return to a lee shore turn head to wind and lower the mainsail before sailing in on a run using the jib alone.

3 | Moorings and Pontoons

Picking up a mooring

In many locations **moorings** are used to provide temporary or permanent berths for keelboats and larger dinghies. A mooring is normally a floating buoy tethered to an anchor on the bottom.

Head for a mooring on a close reach, letting out the sails to slow the boat down as you approach. Turn almost head to wind, stopping alongside the buoy and secure the boat to the buoy. Raise the centreboard, lower the sails and remove the rudder. See diagram A.

In tidal waters, take account of the direction of the current. If wind and tide are in the same direction again, follow diagram A. If wind and tide are opposed, follow diagram B; drop the mainsail and approach under jib alone. Note that you must have enough speed under jib to get over the tide.

Using an engine

Some dinghies and small keelboats have the facility to use an engine. This is usually an outboard that clamps onto a bracket on the transom when needed.

Outboard engines use petrol as fuel and since this is explosive it should be stored in a purpose-built fuel tank. The tank should be kept in a well ventilated locker when not in use, so that any fumes can escape.

When using an outboard engine make sure that it is clamped tightly to its bracket. Check that it is not in gear before you start it and do not use an engine near swimmers or people stood in shallow water. Lower the sails when under power and pull up the centreboard.

Diagram A   *Diagram B*

In sheltered waters a dinghy can be left on a mooring, but the rudder should be removed.

Having the facility to fit an outboard can expand the ways in which you can use your boat and add to your pleasure.

Tying up to a pontoon

A floating **pontoon** can be convenient as a temporary parking place for a dinghy or a permanent home for a keelboat. When approaching a pontoon under sail, come in on a close reach, letting the sails out to slow down the final approach. There are two golden rules when approaching a pontoon:

- Always control your speed to reduce the risk of collision and increase control.

- Plan an escape route so that if you find yourself sailing too fast in the final stages you can sail out and try again.

As you reach the pontoon, turn head to wind to stop. If this is not possible, approach under jib alone.

Secure the boat quickly and lower the sails. Tie the bow and stern to the pontoon.

To leave, hoist the sails, untie the boat, then push the bow off and sail away.

If you sail a keelboat, secure the boat alongside the pontoon using two sets of ropes. The ones from bow and stern, holding the boat close to the pontoon, are called **breast ropes** (1). The others are called **springs** (2) and they stop the boat moving fore and aft. Tie some **fenders** (3) at the widest part of the boat to stop it rubbing against the pontoon.

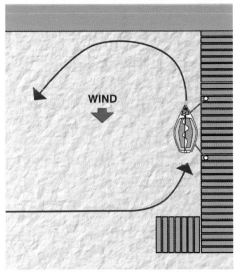

Sail in on a reach and aim to stop head to wind alongside the pontoon. Sail away by pushing off and turning to a reach.

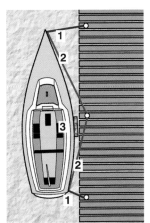

Tie a keelboat to a pontoon using breast ropes (1) and springs (2). Place fenders (3) to prevent damage.

TOP TIP Don't leave your dinghy tied to a pontoon for long as the action of the waves can cause damage to the hull by banging it against the pontoon - always use a fender.

3 | Avoiding Other Boats

Sailing sensibly
Popular sailing areas can get very busy in the summer so it is important to understand the rules for avoiding collisions. They are called the International Regulations for Preventing Collisions At Sea. Your principle duty is to avoid hitting anything; as a beginner it is always better to slow or stop the boat by letting the sheets go and turning into the wind, rather than turning away from the wind which will increase momentum. If you were to hit something at speed it would cause considerably more damage than if the boat were going slowly. A good principle is to keep checking the other boat's course even when you have right of way. If the risk of collision increases, be prepared to take evasive action.

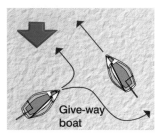

Under sail
'STARBOARD TACK HAS RIGHT OF WAY'
A sailing boat on port tack must keep clear of a boat on starboard tack. If you are on starboard tack, hold your course but be watchful in case the 'port tacker' has not seen you. Remember, you are on a starboard tack if the wind is coming from the right hand side of the boat.

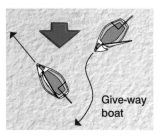

'WINDWARD BOAT KEEPS CLEAR'
When boats are on the same tack, the boat to windward of the other keeps clear. Remember this if you are running towards a boat that is closehauled - you may have to keep clear.

'POWER GIVES WAY TO SAIL'
But beware, it is unrealistic to expect large vessels to give way to a small sailing boat and in many cases it is your duty to give way: use your common sense and take early and clear avoiding action.

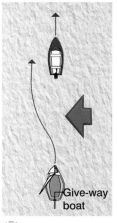

'OVERTAKING BOAT KEEPS CLEAR'
If you are overtaking another boat, you must keep clear, even if you are sailing past a power vessel.

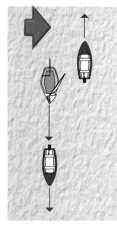

'DRIVE ON THE RIGHT'
When sailing up or down a narrow channel always 'drive on the right' - whether under power or sail - and stay on the right hand side of the channel. If you cross the channel, do so at right angles and give way to all boats following the channel.

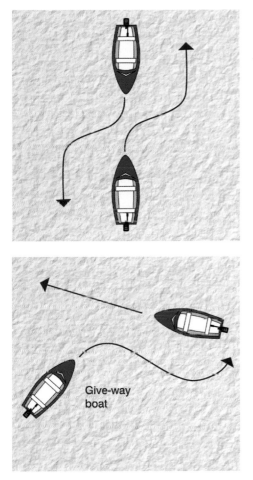

Under power

When rowing, paddling or using the engine you are considered to be under power so be aware of your responsibilities. This applies even if the sails are hoisted.

'POWER BOATS MEETING HEAD-ON'

When two power boats meet head-on they must both turn to starboard so they pass port side to port side.

'POWER BOATS CROSSING'

When two power boats are crossing, the boat on the other's starboard side has right of way. The give way boat must alter course.

Remember, "If you're on the right you're in the right".

Give-way
boat

TOP TIP

Write Port Tack on the port side of your boom, and Starboard Tack on the starboard side. A glance will tell you which tack you are on.

3 | Capsize Recovery

The point of no return for this dinghy crew. They are about to capsize during a gybe - probably because the centreboard is too far down, and they did not move their weight to the new windward side quickly enough as the boom swung across.

Capsizing

Knowing how to deal with a capsize is an important part of learning to sail small boats. At a RYA recognised sailing school, you will be taught how to handle a capsize.

Practice capsizing under controlled conditions. In this way you will learn the simple techniques for righting the boat and gain confidence for dealing with the real situation.

How often you have to recover from a capsize will depend on the type of boat you sail, your level of skill, and the conditions you sail in. Racers will tend to push the limits more frequently than cruisers.

Once you have mastered a recovery technique that works well for your type of boat, a capsize will usually be little more than an inconvenience from which you can quickly recover.

TOP TIP If you find yourself in the water under a sail just put your hand above your head to create an airspace and swim to the edge of the sail.

Righting a two-person boat

The most common type of capsize occurs when the boat heels too much and capsizes to leeward. This type of capsize is relatively slow and gentle. Your buoyancy aid will keep you afloat so relax:

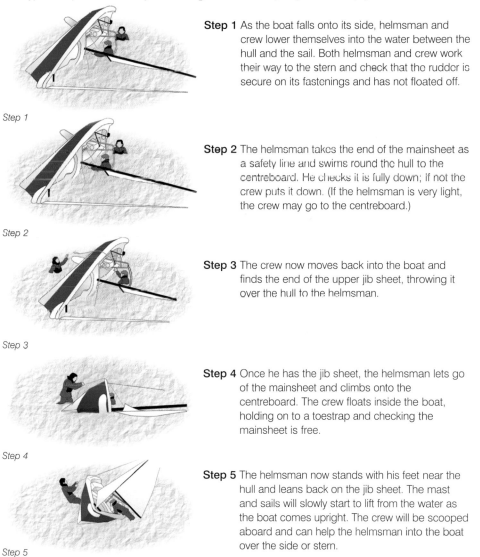

Step 1 As the boat falls onto its side, helmsman and crew lower themselves into the water between the hull and the sail. Both helmsman and crew work their way to the stern and check that the rudder is secure on its fastenings and has not floated off.

Step 1

Step 2 The helmsman takes the end of the mainsheet as a safety line and swims round the hull to the centreboard. He checks it is fully down; If not the crew puts it down. (If the helmsman is very light, the crew may go to the centreboard.)

Step 2

Step 3 The crew now moves back into the boat and finds the end of the upper jib sheet, throwing it over the hull to the helmsman.

Step 3

Step 4 Once he has the jib sheet, the helmsman lets go of the mainsheet and climbs onto the centreboard. The crew floats inside the boat, holding on to a toestrap and checking the mainsheet is free.

Step 4

Step 5 The helmsman now stands with his feet near the hull and leans back on the jib sheet. The mast and sails will slowly start to lift from the water as the boat comes upright. The crew will be scooped aboard and can help the helmsman into the boat over the side or stern.

Step 5

TOP TIP Once modern boats are fully inverted they have no effective air pocket underneath. Stay clear of an inverting boat.

3 | Capsize Recovery

After inversion stand on the edge of the boat and lean back on the centreboard to bring the boat onto its side.

Righting from an inversion

Any boat will turn completely upside down if left on its side for long. This is known as inversion. Some boats are more prone to this than others.

The first step in recovering is to bring the boat back on to its side. Pull yourself onto the upturned hull and stand on the edge while leaning back against the centreboard. If the centreboard has retracted into its case, use a sheet from the other side of the boat to pull against. Now use the standard righting method.

If you have to right an inverted catamaran, sit on the stern of the leeward hull until the opposite bow lifts and the mast starts to come to the surface. As it does so, move to the middle of the lower hull and continue the normal righting process.

Righting a singlehander

Righting a singlehander is easy if you can climb over the high side and onto the centreboard as the boat goes over. From here you can quickly pull the boat upright and climb aboard - staying dry throughout the process. If you fail to climb over the high side or if the boat capsizes to windward, lower yourself gently into the water. Use the mainsheet as a safety line and swim round the hull to the centreboard. To right the boat, pull on the centre board, or climb onto it. As you pull on the side of the hull the boat will right itself and you can climb aboard.

Step 1

Step 2

Step 3

Step 4

Step 1

Step 2

Step 3

Step 4

Step 5

Righting a catamaran

As the catamaran capsizes, slide into the water between the trampoline and the sail. Keep hold of something – the boat may drift quite fast. Once capsized a catamaran can be harder to right than a dinghy, especially if it turns upside down.

Step 1 Move around the front beam to the underside of the boat. Climb onto the hull and throw the righting line over the upper hull. Free the sheets and traveller to prevent the boat sailing away once righted.

Step 2 Turn the boat so that the mast points into wind (the opposite to a dinghy) – the windage of the trampoline and rig will help you right the boat. If necessary, gently depress the bow to swing the hulls around in the breeze

Step 3 Lean back on the righting line (or sheet) to lift the mast tip clear of the water. When the mast lifts clear, the wind will get under the sail, lifting it. The boat will start to right more quickly.

Step 4 Stay under the boat by the front beam as the top hull drops back into the water. Be careful it does not hit you. Grab the front beam as it comes down. This will prevent the boat sailing off or capsizing again.

Step 5 Climb aboard over either beam, check the rudder and sheets and stow any loose lines. Climbing over the lower rear beam is easier if you are tired.

TOP TIP Many boats will drift faster when on their side than you can swim so always keep hold of the boat when you are in the water.

3 | Man Overboard Recovery

First reactions

Man overboard does not happen very often but if it does, you need to know what to do and how to react quickly. If you are sailing a two-person dinghy or catamaran when the other person falls overboard, your first priority is to get the boat under control and to avoid a capsize.

If you are helming and your crew falls overboard let the jib sheet go immediately. If you are crew and the helmsman falls out of the boat, release the jib sheet and grab the tiller to regain control.

If the boat capsizes, you may be close enough for the person in the water to swim to the boat. If not, you must try and right the boat while keeping the person in the water in sight. Do not leave the boat to try and reach them.

Getting back to the man overboard

Once you have the boat under control; steer onto a beam reach and check the position of the person in the water. Let the jib sheet go and ease the mainsail sufficiently to keep the boat upright while retaining enough speed to manoeuvre. Sail away from the person in the water until you have enough room to get downwind of them, ten boat lengths is typical.

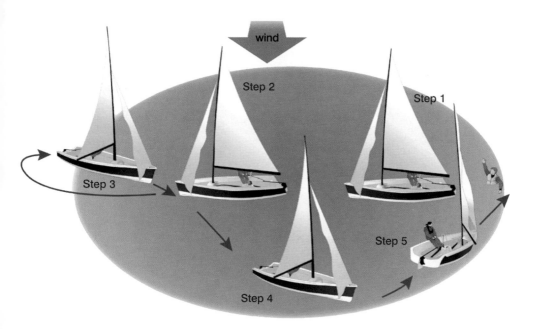

Step 1 Turn to a beam reach and release the jib sheet. Step 2 Sail away until you have room to tack. Step 3 Tack round and Step 4 bear away to a broad reach. Step 5 Approach the person on a close reach letting out the mainsheet to slow you down.

Check that both jib sheets are loose and tack round to the opposite beam reach. Check that you have the person in sight and bear away to a broad reach to get to leeward of him. Make your final approach on a close reach so you can slow down by letting out the mainsheet, without the boom hitting the shroud. The flapping jib is a useful indicator of wind direction. Aim to stop with the person alongside the windward shroud.

In a catamaran you can gybe round to avoid getting stuck in-irons trying to tack. In strong winds aim to stop the boat with the person between the bows. This avoids the boat blowing away from him as it slows down.

Getting the person aboard

As the boat stops alongside the person in the water let the mainsheet run out fully and move forward to grab hold of them. If the boat is still moving it may try to tack around the person in the water so give the tiller extension a tug to windward as you leave it.

To get the person out of the water:

Stop the boat alongside the person in the water so that he can be brought aboard just aft of the shroud, at the widest part of the boat. Depress the side to the water and pull his torso into the boat.

Kneel at the side of the boat and hold the person by their buoyancy aid or under their armpits.

Lean towards them to depress the side of the boat. Now lean backwards and pull their torso over the side.

From here most people can help themselves aboard. If not, have them float alongside the boat, get one of their feet into the boat, then roll their torso aboard horizontally.

In a catamaran bring the person aboard over the forward beam or, if too difficult, over the aft beam where the freeboard is less.

TOP TIP When making the final approach, sail slowly and allow the jib to flap. Luff onto a close reach well before the line of the jib points at the person in the water.

3 | Weather Basics

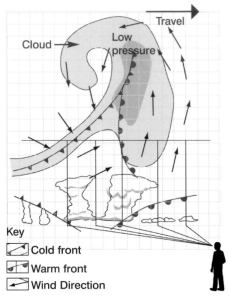

Key

◣ Cold front

◢ Warm front

◂ Wind Direction

Winds circulate anticlockwise around the low. Changes of wind direction occur when warm and cold fronts pass through.

The causes of weather

Weather is a key consideration when you go sailing. Before you go afloat you should know the predicted wind strength and direction, and understand how local effects may alter the forecast. The weather we experience in the UK is caused by the interplay between two types of weather systems: **low pressure** systems (called depressions or lows) and **high pressure** systems (highs or anticyclones).

Low pressure systems travel across the Atlantic and are associated with strong winds, rain and shifting wind direction. They also feature warm and cold **fronts**, the dividing lines between warm and cold air. Fronts are associated with changes in wind direction and often gusty conditions.

High pressure systems are born over land or sea and move more slowly. Highs are generally associated with good weather and light winds.

Understanding local effects

The general wind direction is determined by the location of areas of low and high pressure - the air simply blows from high to low pressure.

With the general direction offshore, the wind is likely to be light inshore and strong further out, but local land features often affect wind direction or strength. For example, the wind will funnel along a river valley and so increase in strength. A high headland will bend the wind so it strengthens just offshore. High land, trees, or tall buildings to windward of the sailing area will create wind shadows (light patches) resulting in shifty and gusty conditions. Get to know the area you sail in and look for geographical and man-made features which will make a difference to the wind pattern.

On hot summer days a **sea breeze** often brings a refreshing onshore wind in the afternoon; but if the sea breeze is combined with the general wind direction the result could be strong conditions and rough sailing.

The sun heats the land faster than the sea. Hot air rises from the land and starts a circulatory system in which the rising hot air is replaced by colder air flowing in from the sea - the sea breeze.

Weather forecasts

You do not need detailed knowledge of weather to go sailing but if you plan to go to the coast, it is wise to get a forecast.

Check the forecast for wind strength and direction as well as poor visibility or fog (often a problem on Britain's coastline). Good sources of information include radio, television, phone and fax in addition to numerous websites. Detailed marine forecasts are now available by phone.

Judging wind strength

Wind strength is described in the Beaufort Scale below. Learn to recognise the strength of the wind by what you see ashore and afloat.

TOP TIP Check out the local weather forecast before you go sailing and ask advice from experienced locals if you are not sure about the conditions.

Force	Wind Speed	Description	Signs on Land	Effects on Sea
0	Less than 1 knot	Calm	Flags hang limply, leaves do not move on trees, smoke rises vertically.	Glassy sea, boats drift with limp sails. Heel the boat to leeward a little to help the sail hold their shape. Move gently and slowly in the boat.
1	1-3 knots	Light Air	Light flags start to stir and smoke drifts away from vertical.	Small catspaws and ripples on surface and sails fill. Sit forward in the boat and allow it to heel slightly to keep sails full. Move gently in the boat
2	4-6 knots	Light Breeze	Flags start to indicate wind direction and leaves rustle on trees.	Steady light wind for sailing. Boats are still underpowered but can be sailed upright. Use smooth movements during manoeuvres to maintain speed.
3	7-10 knots	Gentle Breeze	Flags extend outwards but remain below horizontal from the flagstaff.	Ideal conditions for learning to sail. Small waves form and most small boats sail efficiently with full power available from the sails.
4	11-15 knots	Moderate Breeze	Small branches move on trees, and flags are fully extended horizontally. Small pieces of paper blow along the ground.	Waves have foaming tops. Crews have to work hard to balance dinghies and catamarans. Beginners should reef or head for shore.
5	16-21 knots	Fresh Breeze	The tops of large trees move and small trees sway. Flags are extended slightly above horizontal.	Good conditions for experienced crews but capsizes are common. Inexperienced sailors should stay ashore.
6	22-27 knots	Strong Breeze	Wind whistles through telephone lines and large trees sway. Flags blow above horizontal.	Experienced crews may sail but only if good safety cover is available.

3 | Sailing in Coastal Waters

Sailing in coastal waters offers the freedom to explore new areas - but be aware of tidal movements. Ensure that your boat is seaworthy and carries sufficient safety equipment.

Safety matters

Coastal waters provide some wonderful sailing venues with the opportunity for good racing or day sailing. You will face the challenge of sailing in tides and on open water. Waves develop quickly on the sea when the wind reaches Force 3 or more, and you may be much further from shore and safety cover.

Before you go afloat in coastal waters check the weather forecast for several hours ahead and ensure that the conditions will be within your capabilities. Also check the time of high and low water, and find out the direction of the tidal stream during the time you plan to be sailing. You can find the time of high and low water in a local tide table, and the direction of the tidal stream from a pilot guide, tidal atlas, or chart of the area.

If you are in any doubt, ask an experienced local sailor for advice. Tell a reliable person of your plans and the time you expect to be back so they can notify the rescue services if you do not return on time.

Causes of tides

Tides are caused by gravitational pull on the earth by the moon and sun. **Spring** tides occur about every fortnight - when the sun and moon are in line at the times of the full and new moon. They feature the highest high tides and the lowest low tides.

In between spring tides there are **neap** tides, when the moon is in its first and last quarter. During neap tides there is less height difference between high and low tide (**tidal range**).

Tidal streams are stronger during spring tides and weaker at neap tides.

Strong tides occur in some coastal waters. The wake around a buoy shows strength and direction; here the tidal stream is running from right to left.

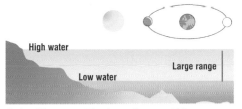

High water
Low water
Large range

Spring tides occur at the times of new and full moon. The difference in height between high and low tide (tidal range) is at its greatest.

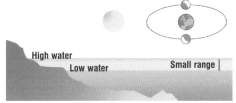

High water
Low water
Small range

Neap tides occur at the moon's first and last quarter. The difference in height between high and low tide (tidal range) is at its least.

Sailing in tides

When you sail in coastal waters take the effect of the tide into account. Find out the tide's direction before you go afloat and remember that it is likely to change in strength and direction while you are sailing.

Plan to have the tide with you when you head for home to make the return journey easier and to allow for a deterioration in the weather.

Conditions will be rougher than usual for the strength of the wind if the wind blows against a strong tidal stream.

TOP TIP

To sail a straight course across a tidal stream or current, line up two fixed objects ahead of you on the shore and keep them in line.

3 | Starting to Race

Where to race

One of the best ways to develop your new-found sailing skills is to start racing.

Most clubs organise racing for their members and visitors. Many dinghy, keelboat and catamaran classes organise Open Meetings where you can race against some of the top sailors in your class.

To start with, visit your local sailing club and find someone who needs a crew.

If you have your own boat join a club that offers racing for the class.

Types of race courses

Many different courses can be set to suit the type of boats and local conditions. Dinghies, catamarans and small keelboats often sail a sausage course, featuring a series of upwind and downwind legs, but there are also triangular or square courses.

Details of the course will be found in the sailing instructions, together with details on starting signals, special rules etc.

Racing can help to improve your skills in strong conditions when you might not otherwise go out without the safety cover provided by the club that organises the racing.

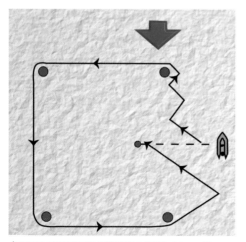

A square course tests sailing on a reach, run, and to windward.

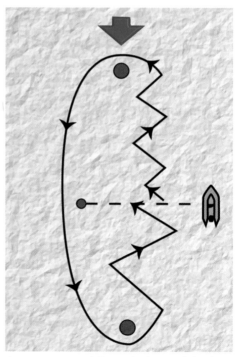

A sausage course puts the emphasis on upwind and downwind sailing.

Starting procedures

The start line will usually be laid at right angles to the wind, often between a committee boat and a small buoy.

The race officer will display flags or coloured boards and make sound signals to indicate the course and the countdown to the start.

Unless the sailing instructions specify otherwise, there will be a warning signal five minutes before the start, followed by a preparatory signal at four minutes to go, a one minute signal, and the starting signal.

Races for popular classes often have crowded start lines but when you start racing it is likely to be in smaller fleets with less intense competition.

Sailing the course

For your first few races don't worry if you are left behind by the rest of the fleet - it will take you a little while to understand how to start on time and how to sail at maximum speed. The start and the first leg are of crucial importance. If you get round the first mark near the front of the fleet, it will be easier to stay in touch throughout the race.

Practise sailing up to an improvised start line until you can hit the line at full speed on the starting signal. The first leg of the course is nearly always set to windward. It is here that your skill at sailing closehauled will be tested.

If you find that you are sailing slowly compared to other boats around you, look at how they have their sails set and the way they sail their boats and try to copy them.

TOP TIP

Join a club that races dinghies, keelboats, or catamarans and get some experience crewing for others before you buy your own boat.

3 | Staying Safe

Safety equipment

Sailing is generally a very safe sport but it is important to carry the appropriate safety equipment and know how to summon assistance   if necessary. The type and amount of gear you need will depend on the boat you sail and where you go afloat. A paddle to get you home if the wind drops may suffice if you sail on inland waters.

If you sail on coastal waters, carry an anchor with sufficient line in case of a breakdown or lack of wind. Folding anchors are the easiest to stow on a small boat.

 If your boat is fitted with an engine or gas-fuelled cooking equipment you should have a fire extinguisher on board.

A small first aid kit stowed in a waterproof container is useful in case an injury needs treatment before you can get ashore. Whatever equipment you carry, keep it in good condition and make sure that you know how to use it.

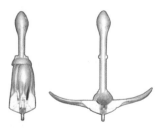

An anchor is essential if you sail on the sea and can also be useful inland.

A simple first aid kit is a sensible item of safety gear.

Carry a fire extinguisher if your boat has gas or petrol on board.

A paddle, or a pair of oars, are vital items when the wind drops.

How to summon help

If a situation develops beyond the point where you can deal with it, seek outside assistance. If you sail on inland waters you may be able to attract attention by shouting. If you sail on coastal waters carry flares and keep them dry. Read the instructions and explain to your crew how to use the flares before the need arises.

Flares are used to attract attention when you need assistance.

If you need assistance and have no flares, raise and lower your extended arms.

Promoting and Protecting Boating
www.rya.org.uk

1 Important To help us comply with Data Protection legislation, please tick *either* Box A or Box B (you must tick Box A to ensure you receive the full benefits of RYA membership). The RYA will not pass your data to third parties.

☐ **A.** I wish to join the RYA and receive future information on member services, benefits (as listed in RYA Magazine and website) and offers.

☐ **B.** I wish to join the RYA but do not wish to receive future information on member services, benefits (as listed in RYA Magazine and website) and offers.

When completed, please send this form to: RYA, RYA House, Ensign Way, Hamble, Southampton, SO31 4YA

2

	Title	Forename	Surname	Date of Birth		Male	Female
				D D / M M / Y Y		☐	☐
1.				D D / M M / Y Y		☐	☐
2.				D D / M M / Y Y		☐	☐
3.				D D / M M / Y Y		☐	☐
4.							

Address

Town   County   Post Code

Evening Telephone   Daytime Telephone

email

Signature: Date:

3 Type of membership required: *(Tick Box)*

☐ **Personal** From 1 October 2007 annual rate £39 or £36 by Direct Debit

☐ **Under 21** From 1 October 2007 annual rate £13 (no reduction for Direct Debit)

☐ **Family*** From 1 October 2007 annual rate £58 or £54 by Direct Debit

* Family Membership: 2 adults plus any under 21s all living at the same address

4 Please tick ONE box to show your main boating interest.

☐ Yacht Racing   ☐ Yacht Cruising
☐ Dinghy Racing   ☐ Dinghy Cruising
☐ Personal Watercraft   ☐ Inland Waterways
☐ Powerboat Racing   ☐ Windsurfing
☐ Motor Boating   ☐ Sportsboats and RIBs

Please see Direct Debit form overleaf

![RYA logo]

Instructions to your Bank or Building Society to pay by Direct Debit

Please complete this form and return it to:
Royal Yachting Association, RYA House, Ensign Way, Hamble, Southampton, Hampshire SO31 4YA

Originators Identification Number

9	5	5	2	1	3

To The Manager: Bank/Building Society

Address:

Post Code:

2. Name(s) of account holder(s)

3. Branch Sort Code

	—			—		

4. Bank or Building Society account number

Banks and Building Societies may not accept Direct Debit instructions for some types of account

Cash, Cheque, Postal Order enclosed £
Made payable to the Royal Yachting Association

077 Office use only: Membership Number Allocated

5. RYA Membership Number (For office use only)

6. Instruction to pay your Bank or Building Society

Please pay Royal Yachting Association Direct Debits from the account detailed in this instruction subject to the safeguards assured by The Direct Debit Guarantee.
I understand that this instruction may remain with the Royal Yachting Association and, if so, details will be passed electronically to my Bank/Building Society.

Signature(s)

Date

Office use / Centre Stamp